D0875969

# ELECTRICITY

HISTORY OF SCIENCE

# ELECTRICITY

## FROM FARADAY TO
## SOLAR GENERATORS
### BY MARTIN J. GUTNIK

A GROLIER COMPANY

FRANKLIN WATTS
NEW YORK • LONDON • TORONTO
SYDNEY • 1986

Library of Congress Cataloging
in Publication Data

Gutnik, Martin J.
Electricity : from Faraday
to solar generators.

(History of science)
Includes index.
Summary: Traces the history of the study of
electricity, from discoveries by the early
Greeks to more recent developments in commu-
nication, electronics, and solar generators.
1. Electricity—History—Juvenile literature.
2. Electric power production—History—
Juvenile literature. [1. Electricity—History]
I. Title II. Series: History of science
(Franklin Watts, Inc.)
QC507.G8 1986       537'.09       86-11130
ISBN 0-531-10222-X

To my friend
and colleague
Fred Bolliger

Diagrams by Vantage Art, Inc.

Photographs courtesy of
Culver Pictures, Inc.:
pp. 14, 43, 47, 70;
The Granger Collection:
pp. 20 (top left and bottom right),
21 (top right and bottom left),
28, 36, 40, 50, 74;
The Bettmann Archive: p. 20
(top right and bottom left);
F. Scott Barr Collection/AIP Niels
Bohr Library: p. 21 (top left);
Deutsches Museum/AIP Niels
Bohr Library: p. 21 (bottom right);
AIP/Niels Bohr Library: p. 31.

# CONTENTS

# ELECTRICITY

# THE BIRTH OF A SCIENCE

It was the Greeks who first used the terms *electricity* and *magnetism*. Magnetism is not electricity, but its history and use are so intertwined with electricity that one cannot study electricity without a knowledge of magnetism.

One of the first discoveries relating to electricity was made thousands of years ago, when people first realized that the iron ore magnetite—a dark, shiny, crystal-like material—has the ability to attract and repel other objects. People called these pieces of magnetite *lodestones.* In China, lodestones were used by travelers to find their way. They knew that if a piece of iron was rubbed against a lodestone, the iron, when suspended on a string, would always point in the same direction. This was the world's first *compass.*

In a different part of the world, about fifteen hundred years later, the Greek philosopher Thales discovered a resin called amber. Experimenting with both lodestones and amber, he found that lodestones attracted heavy objects, such as nails or needles, while rubbed amber attracted light objects, such as feathers or parchment.

The Greek word for amber is *elektron.* The word electricity comes from this Greek word, because electricity is electrons in motion.

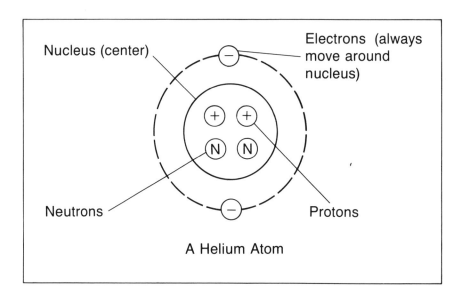

Nucleus (center)

Electrons (always move around nucleus)

Neutrons

Protons

A Helium Atom

Electrons are very small, negatively charged particles (a particle with an excess of electrons), that are found in *atoms.* An atom is one of the smallest particles that make up matter. Atoms have three particles: *protons* and *neutrons,* found in the center (nucleus) of the atom; and *electrons,* which orbit the nucleus. The movement of electrons is electricity. All objects are made up of atoms. In static electricity, objects rubbed together lose electrons to other objects.

Atoms contain other particles. These particles are found in the nucleus (center) of the atom and do not move. One of these particles is a proton, positively charged; and the other is a neutron, which possesses no electrical charge.

## EUROPE AWAKES

In the year 1600, the first breakthrough appeared in the study of magnetism and electricity. An English physician by the name of

William Gilbert (1544-1603) spent years experimenting with magnetism and electricity. He published a book about his work, *On the Loadstone and Magnetic Bodies and on the Great Magnet, the Earth.* In his book he explained how Earth itself is a magnet, and went on to explain how a compass works.

Gilbert related how he believed amber attracts and repels different materials. He explained how he had rubbed amber against a cloth, and then how this rubbed amber attracted light materials. Gilbert believed that the *force* possessed by amber was not magnetism but, rather, electricity. Amber, Gilbert said, "electrifies" certain materials, and this causes them to be attracted to the amber. Gilbert was the first person to distinguish between electricity and magnetism, and the first European to use the term "electricity."

Another Englishman, Robert Boyle (1627-1691), experimented with static electricity. He discovered that electricity would appear when a solid piece of sulfur was rubbed with cloth.

## THE FIRST ELECTRICAL GENERATING MACHINE

Otto von Guericke (1602-1686), in Germany, was familiar with Gilbert's and Boyle's observations about electricity and its effects. In 1660, von Guericke carried out his own experiment with static electricity. He made a large ball of sulfur and mounted it on a wooden frame. He used sulfur because it was readily available and had static electric properties. He spun the ball with a crank, and held a piece of soft cloth against the ball while it rotated. When the cloth made contact with the sulfur ball, sparks shot out in all directions. These sparks were electricity.

Von Guericke also discovered that electricity has the ability to attract and repel certain objects. He held a feather close to the spinning globe of sulfur and saw that it was attracted to the ball, yet, as soon as the feather touched the globe, it was repelled and floated above the spinning ball.

William Gilbert, physician to Queen Elizabeth I of England, demonstrates his theories on magnetism and electricity to the queen and members of her court.

# PROPERTIES OF
# ELECTRICITY

Many years after von Guericke's death, Stephen Gray (1695-1736), an Englishman, discovered that certain objects will carry an electrical charge while others will not. He made this observation when he discovered how to transmit an electrical charge (make electricity move). Objects that allow passage of an electrical charge are *conductors,* and objects that do not allow passage of an electrical charge are insulators, or nonconductors.

Gray transmitted an electrical charge from a glass tube to an iron rod by using a wire. He was one of the first people to use a wire as an electrical conductor. Gray also discovered that electrical charges do not penetrate an object's interior but are held on the object's surface.

Gray's discoveries stimulated other scientists, like the Frenchman Charles Du Fay (1698-1739), to work with the conduction of electricity. Du Fay demonstrated that all objects could be electrified. He also discovered the difference between the two kinds of electricity, static and current. *Static electricity* is electricity created by friction when certain objects are rubbed together. *Current electricity* is electrons moving through a conductor.

In a fledgling nation across the ocean, Benjamin Franklin (1706-1790), too, was experimenting with static and current electricity. Franklin's kite experiment demonstrated that lightning is electricity.

Benjamin Franklin was the first to use the terms *positive charge* and *negative charge.* Du Fay had said that electricity consists of two fluids, resinous and vitreous. Franklin said there is only one electrical force, which has two aspects: a positive part (excess) and a negative part (a deficiency). The terms that Franklin coined are still in use, but today they have different meanings. Although Franklin believed the positive to be an excess, it is really the deficiency. Positive means a lack of electrons. Negative means an excess of (too many) electrons.

Franklin also believed that a pointed object has more ability to attract an electrical charge than a round one. In order to prove his theory, Franklin set up a pointed conductor on a building with the point skyward. His belief was that lightning charges would be attracted to this conductor. His theory proved to be correct. During a storm, lightning struck the conductor, and its electrical charge was carried safely into the ground by an attached wire. This was the first lightning rod. Today lightning rods are not necessarily pointed because modern research has shown that the point is not needed.

In 1785, Charles Augustin de Coulomb (1736-1806), a French scientist, discovered the laws of attraction and repulsion (like charges repel; unlike charges attract) between electrically charged bodies. In honor of his discovery, the unit of electrical charge, the coulomb, is named for him.

De Coulomb's discovery marked the end of an era of discovery in static electricity. The scientific community now turned its attentions to electrons in motion, or current electricity.

## ELECTRONS IN MOTION

It was Luigi Galvani (1737-1798), an Italian physician and physicist, who first observed the effect of electric current, and it was by accident. As professor of anatomy at the University of Bologna, Galvani was studying the effects of irritation on the nerves. He used frogs for his experiments.

It was while conducting an experiment on a dissected frog that Galvani made his monumental observation. The frog lay on a table next to an electric machine that was producing electrons. When one of Galvani's assistants happened to touch the frog's nerve with a scalpel, the frog's legs kicked out. Galvani concluded that the electrons from the machine traveled through the scalpel to the nerve and caused this reaction.

Galvani pursued this idea by performing other experiments. He attached frogs' legs to an iron railing with a copper hook. The frogs' legs twitched whenever they touched the iron railing. Galvani's experiments led him to believe that electricity was in the muscles or nerves of animals. He called this his theory of animal electricity.

Many scientists tested Galvani's theory until an Italian natural history professor, Alessandro Volta (1745-1827), discovered why the frogs' legs twitched. Volta stated that the electricity was not in the muscles or nerves of the frogs' legs but in the chemical action between two different metals, copper and iron.

Volta, after proving Galvani's theory wrong, continued his research into the electrical interaction of metals. He tested many metals and charted their interactions. Volta believed that the electrical charge came from the contact of the two metals. But, in order to get a better electrical connection, Volta moistened pieces of cloth with brine (salt water) and placed the cloth between the two different types of metals. This, he knew, would increase the electrical charge. In order to increase the charge, he piled up different metal discs with brine-soaked cloth in between them. This eventually led to his invention of the *voltaic pile,* in 1796 (see page 18). Volta had discovered a way in which to produce a continuous flow of electricity. His voltaic pile was the first source of direct current electricity, the first battery.

Volta himself did not realize the great potential of his discovery. He did not foresee his voltaic pile as the invention that would enable more extensive experiments in electricity.


## HUMPHRY DAVY

Sir Humphry Davy (1778-1829), an English chemist, was impressed with Volta's pile and excited about its potential for further experimentation in electricity. The pile could do what nothing else could before—provide a continuous flow of electricity. Volta believed that electricity from his pile came from the interaction of the metals contacting, or touching, one another. He called this his contact theory.

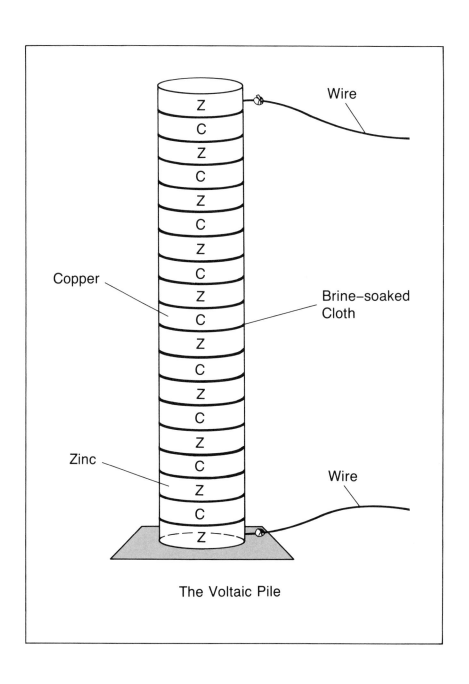

Wire

Copper

Brine-soaked Cloth

Zinc

Wire

The Voltaic Pile

Humphry Davy supported Volta's contact theory. Many of Europe's scientists agreed with Volta and Davy, but many did not. An opposing theory—the chemical theory—was later put forth by Michael Faraday (1791-1867).

Faraday (and others) believed the electricity in the voltaic pile came from chemical action, not contact. The chemical theory stated that the zinc was eaten away by chemical action, producing hydrogen gas. This hydrogen gas bubbled out at the copper. It was the release of this hydrogen gas that produced the flow of electricity.

The argument between the contact and chemical theories lasted forty years. Eventually it became clear that Faraday and his followers were correct.

Humphry Davy was trained as a physician-apothecary, intending to enter the medical profession. After making several speeches on medicine at the Medical Pneumatic Institution in Bristol, Davy was invited to become a lecturer and director of London's Royal Institution, which had been established by Count Rumford for research into the sciences. Davy became a professor there.

One of Davy's first experiments at the Royal Institution was to work on the further development of Volta's pile. In his researches, Davy developed a battery made from over 200 zinc and cop-

*Over: What electrical terms or measurements come to mind when you hear the names of these scientists? (a) William Gilbert, (b) Luigi Galvani, (c) Charles Augustin de Coulomb, (d) Alessandro Volta, (e) André Marie Ampère, (f) Hans Christian Oersted, (g) Georg Simon Ohm, (h) Heinrich Hertz.*

(C)

(D)

(G)

(H)

per plate couplings. He used this battery to perform electrical experiments.

In 1801, Davy used his battery to produce the *electric arc,* a luminous flame of electricity that leaps from one conductor to another. This arc, whose conductors are made from carbon contacts, created a brilliant light. Davy's arc served as the prototype for the carbon arc light and the electric furnace.

Davy also used his battery to perform experiments in *electrolysis.* Electrolysis is the passing of electric current through a liquid, causing the decomposition of the solution. Davy also used his battery to melt solids. In doing this, he discovered that he could break down compounds into their separate elements. By applying this theory, Davy revealed the elements potassium, sodium, strontium, and many other previously unknown elements.

Davy's findings were a major contribution to people's knowledge of current electricity. Under the sponsorship of the Royal Institution, Davy was able to experiment freely. All of Europe was now alive with the excitement of electricity. It was an age of discovery, a time of great change, as people began to search for scientific answers to natural phenomena. It was in this atmosphere that research into electromagnetism went forward.

CHAPTER

# 2

## FROM
## ELECTROMAGNETISM
## TO INDUCTION

By the end of the eighteenth century, many similarities between electricity and magnetism were known. Scientists realized that both electricity and magnetism followed the same laws of force and, in many respects, seemed to display the same properties. Yet, although these similarities were known to exist, the relationship between the two phenomena was not understood. Each field was studied separately and separate laws were developed. It was not until 1820, with the publication of Hans Christian Oersted's findings, that the relationship between electricity and magnetism was recognized.

## THE SWING OF
## A COMPASS NEEDLE

Hans Christian Oersted (1777-1851) was the self-educated son of a Danish pharmacist. Through hard work and study, he was accepted at the University of Copenhagen, where he received a doctor's degree in metaphysics and became a professor of natural philosophy. In 1806, he was appointed professor of physics at the University of Copenhagen.

Oersted traveled a great deal in order to learn more about the startling new discoveries in electricity. It was in 1812, while traveling in Germany and France, that he expressed the belief that magnetism was associated with electricity. He thought about ways that static electricity (galvanism) might affect a magnet.

In 1819, while lecturing on the heating effects of voltaic electricity, Oersted made his greatest discovery. During the lecture, a compass lay near his electrical apparatus. He noticed that the needle of the compass seemed to move with the opening and closing of the electric circuit. He wondered why.

After the lecture, Oersted tried the experiment again. Yes, there was a definite swing of the compass needle. When the current was on, it swung one way, and when the current was off, it swung back. He tried again, and this time found not only that the current traveling through the wire deflected the compass needle, but also that the wire seemed to be deflected by the magnet.

Oersted discovered that a current of electricity creates a magnetic field. He demonstrated for the first time the connection between electricity and magnetism. He published his discoveries in 1820, and soon his work inspired other scientists to further experiments.


## IN THE FOOTSTEPS
## OF OERSTED

François Jean Arago (1786-1853), a French scientist, building on Oersted's discoveries, found that the current flowing in the wire would magnetize previously unmagnetized iron filings. André Marie Ampère (1775-1836) showed that current-carrying wires affect each other, and that wires with current flowing in the same direction attract one another. He also showed that a coil of wire with current flowing through it acts exactly like a magnet. It was this discovery that eventually would pave the way for the development of the electric motor and generator.

Ampère formulated many laws which set the standards for modern magnetic theory. He measured and calculated the magnetic forces generated by electric currents. Two other French scientists, Jean Baptiste Biot (1774-1862) and Felix Savart (1791-1841), worked out mathematical laws governing the force of magnetism between current-carrying objects.

As well as stimulating scientific thought and discovery, Oersted's work brought about the development of an instrument called the *galvanometer.* Galvanometers detect an electric current from its magnetic effect. An electric current passing through a galvanometer creates a magnetic field that causes the needle of the instrument to turn at right angles to its former direction. A simple galvanometer consists of several turns of wire mounted over a compass.

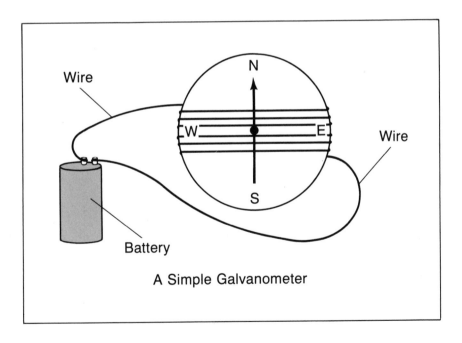

A Simple Galvanometer

Georg Simon Ohm (1787-1854), a German scientist, developed Ohm's law, which establishes a mathematical relationship between current, voltage, and resistance. Resistance can be compared to friction. As the electrons move through a conductor, they rub against one another. This rubbing slows them down and creates heat. Ohm's law states: the larger the resistance, the smaller the current; the greater the electrical push, the greater the current.

All of these men—Ampère, Davy, Ohm, and others—were stimulated by Oersted's discovery. Electromagnetism was a giant step toward even more important discoveries.

It was one of Davy's assistants, Michael Faraday (1791-1867), who made one of the most significant discoveries in the history of electricity: *electromagnetic induction.*

# A GENIUS NAMED FARADAY

The scientist who was to play the major role in harnessing the power of electricity was born on September 22, 1791, into a poor family living in a suburb of London. At the age of thirteen, Michael Faraday quit school and went to work as apprentice to a bookbinder named Riebau.

Faraday lived and worked in Mr. Riebau's shop. During his apprenticeship, he learned how to assemble the pages of a book in their proper order, sew them together, and bind them with a leather cover. But Faraday, having a very curious nature and an uncontrollable desire to learn, also read almost every book he bound. He read before work, during his lunch break, and after work. He read until all hours of the night, and made notes on everything he read. He organized these notes and bound them in a notebook.

Mr. Riebau was impressed with Faraday's desire to learn and encouraged his reading. He often gave his apprentice books to bind that he knew Faraday would be interested in reading, books on science.

Faraday converted his bedroom above the shop into a make-shift laboratory. Here he would read books, such as the *Encyclopedia Britannica*, and then perform experiments to verify his

readings. He was fascinated with electricity and read everything he could find on the subject. He performed his experiments with materials he purchased and with metal scraps from the shop. He often showed his experiments to a much impressed Mr. Riebau.

Mr. Riebau asked if he could read the notebook that Faraday kept on his experiments and readings. Faraday agreed, and gave his cherished notes to the bookbinder. After reading the notes, Riebau passed the book on to a customer, a Mr. Dance.

## A FATEFUL MEETING

Mr. Dance, a wealthy man with a strong interest in the sciences, was favorably impressed with Faraday's work and asked to meet the young man. He gave Faraday tickets to hear the lectures of Humphry Davy at the Royal Institution.

There were four lectures on electricity and Faraday attended every one. He took extensive notes. After the lectures, he would return to his room, where he recopied the notes he had taken onto clean paper and drew pictures of the experiments Davy had performed. Faraday then bound the recopied notes together and made them into a thick book.

In book form, the notes were easier to study. Faraday loved studying, and he studied the notes, attempting to learn as much as he could.

At the age of twenty-one, Faraday reached the end of his apprenticeship and was a journeyman bookbinder. He took a job in the shop of another bookbinder. The work was boring, and Faraday was quite unhappy. He wanted to be a philosopher. (In the 1800s, scientists were considered philosophers.)

*Michael Faraday*

It was around this time that Faraday wrote a letter to Humphry Davy, asking him for a job at the Royal Institution. Along with the letter, Faraday sent the notes he had taken on Davy's lectures.

Davy was impressed with Faraday's letter and especially with his notes. He requested that the young man come to his office for an interview. Davy told Faraday that his bound notebook demonstrated that he had the organization and discipline to become a philosopher-scientist but, Davy went on, science is a harsh master and a career in science can be very frustrating. He said that Faraday was better off being a bookbinder. Besides, Davy explained, there were no positions available at the Royal Institution.

Faraday was very disappointed when he left the meeting with Davy. But, several months later, Davy was injured in an accident in his laboratory, and sent for Faraday to come to the Institution to write letters for him. Faraday did, and several months after this, Davy asked Faraday to become his assistant.


CHALLENGING GIANTS

In 1816, Michael Faraday became a lecturer, speaking to members of the City Philosophical Society on many scientific subjects. He was becoming well-known by members of the scientific community, and his thoughts were greatly respected by others.

It was Oersted's discovery of electromagnetism that prompted Faraday to move away from chemistry, a subject of particular interest to him, to concentrate his efforts in the field of electricity. In 1820, Faraday performed Oersted's experiment in his laboratory at the Royal Institution. He repeated the experiment several times and, after each time, he analyzed the results. Why, he wondered, does the compass jump in one direction when the battery is connected to the wire and in the other direction when the wire is disconnected?

Oersted believed that the movement of the compass needle in this manner was caused by the electric current. This current,

*Faraday's laboratory at the Royal Institution*

Oersted hypothesized, produced circles of force around the wire. The Danish scientist's theory was based on Ampère's law, which stated that the magnetic force of an electric current is around the wire.

Faraday wrote a paper entitled "History of the Progress of Electromagnetism." In this paper he questioned Oersted's and Ampère's theories. Faraday stated that if there were electrical circles of force around a wire, then why wouldn't the same thing be true for a magnet? And, if this idea were correct, then why wouldn't objects move in circles about a magnet?

With these thoughts in mind, Faraday decided to investigate the possibilities of producing rotation by magnetic interaction. Faraday believed that electric current could produce rotation (circular motion) of a magnet's poles around a conducting wire.

On September 3, 1821, Faraday made his first great discovery. He arranged a magnet upright in a dish of mercury with a wire hanging from a pivot above. The magnet was secured with paraffin wax, which was surrounded by the mercury in the dish. The end of the pivoted wire was dipped into the mercury, and was free to move about the magnet.

With this equipment in place, an electric current was passed through the wire, the circuit being completed by the mercury. Faraday believed that when the circuit was completed the conducting wire would be driven in a circle about the magnet.

The experiment was successful, and proved that a magnetic force field will make a wire move in a circle around a magnet's pole. It is the push and pull (force) of the magnet's field that makes the wire move.

The electrically charged wire possesses magnetic properties. It acts like a magnet. The poles of the wire are repelled by the like poles of the magnet and, therefore, cause the wire to move away. This repulsion and attraction are what cause the rotation.

Faraday's experiment was a giant step in electrical science. He did not know it then, but his discovery of electromagnetic rotation was the forerunner of the electric motor.

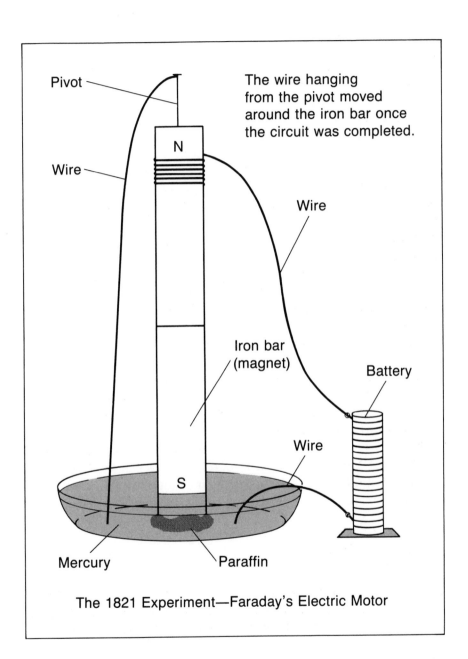

Pivot

Wire

The wire hanging
from the pivot moved
around the iron bar once
the circuit was completed.

N

Wire

Iron bar
(magnet)

Battery

Wire

S

Mercury

Paraffin

The 1821 Experiment—Faraday's Electric Motor

## FIELD THEORY

Most of Faraday's discoveries are related to his idea of matter as fields of force. An object, any object, is not affected by the forces of other objects but by its own forces. According to Faraday, all objects possess fields of force. It is the interaction of each object's individual force with another's that causes electricity.

In making the electric motor, Faraday put his theories to the test. The pivot wire over the magnet is the center of its own force. When the electric current is passed through a wire, the forces of the wire interact with the force of the magnet. The wire's positive forces are repelled by the magnet's positive forces, while attracted to the magnet's negative forces. It is this interaction, the attraction and repulsion, that causes the wire to move in a circular motion about the magnet.

Faraday was one of the first scientists to challenge Sir Isaac Newton's laws of gravitational forces. Newton (1642-1727) said forces can only act on bodies. For example, the force of gravity acts on the body of every object on Earth. Faraday did not believe this to be true. He said that forces act on forces, not bodies.

Faraday also believed that forces can be transferred or converted to other forces. This belief stimulated him to disagree with Volta. Volta stated that the electricity in his pile came from contact between the metals, whereas Faraday believed the electricity was caused by the forces of the chemicals interacting, and that when this chemical action was used up, the electricity ceased. Faraday's theory, some forty years after the controversy began, was proven to be correct.


## ELECTROMAGNETIC INDUCTION

In 1825, an Englishman named William Sturgeon (1783-1850) produced the first *electromagnet*. An electromagnet is a magnet that works by an electrical current being passed around it. A piece of iron is wrapped in wire and, where the electric current goes through the wire, it magnetizes the iron.

Sturgeon's magnet was a piece of iron bent into a horseshoe shape, with sixteen turns of wire wrapped around it, but not touching one another. When current was passed through the wire, the magnet could hold up objects as heavy as nine pounds (4 kg).

Sturgeon's experiments stimulated Faraday in his thinking that magnetism could produce electricity. All the research going on at the time pointed to the correctness of Faraday's theories. Newton had said there is action and there is reaction. Faraday knew the chemical action in a battery would produce electricity and electricity would produce chemical action. He believed all things in the world affect each other and are affected by one another. Thus, if magnetism can be produced by electricity, then electricity can be produced by magnetism.

In one of Faraday's first attempts to produce electricity from magnetism, *electromagnetic induction*, he set up an elaborate apparatus made up of a wooden spool wound with twelve spirals of wire insulated by calico and twine. He connected the even-numbered coils into a series and the odd-numbered coils into another series. He connected one series to a battery and the other series to a galvanometer. On his first attempt with this setup, he saw no effect on the galvanometer. Thinking there was no reaction because the battery was too weak, he substituted a more powerful battery and tried again. On the second attempt there was no noticeable effect on the galvanometer while the current flowed through the wires, but when the current was discontinued (when the circuit was broken), the needle of the galvanometer deflected.

Faraday performed the experiment again. This time he noticed that the galvanometer deflected when the circuit was first made and when it was broken. These deflections were so small that it is a wonder that Faraday even noticed them. Faraday analyzed what this meant. When there was no current or a steady

# EXPERIMENTAL RESEARCHES

IN

# ELECTRICITY.

BY

## MICHAEL FARADAY, D.C.L. F.R.S.

FULLERIAN PROFESSOR OF CHEMISTRY IN THE ROYAL INSTITUTION.

CORRESPONDING MEMBER, ETC., OF THE ROYAL AND IMPERIAL ACADEMIES OF
SCIENCE OF PARIS, PETERSBURGH, FLORENCE, COPENHAGEN, BERLIN,
GOTTINGEN, MODENA, STOCKHOLM, PALERMO, ETC., ETC.

Reprinted from the Philosophical Transactions of 1831—1838.

LONDON:

RICHARD AND JOHN EDWARD TAYLOR,

PRINTERS AND PUBLISHERS TO THE UNIVERSITY OF LONDON,

RED LION COURT, FLEET STREET.

1839.

current in the battery coil, there was no induced electricity; but when the current was started or stopped, there was induced electricity. For the first time ever, an electric current had been produced through magnetic interaction.

Faraday reasoned that the electricity was induced when there was a change in the lines of magnetic force. It was the production and the destruction of the lines of force that caused the current in a nearby circuit. In other words, as long as the lines of force were constant, no current could be produced, but when the lines of force were created or stopped, an electric current was induced. This was the start of induction theory.

## FARADAY'S DYNAMO

Faraday continued to experiment to perfect the induction of electricity. He wanted to be able to generate a constant electric current. He attempted this by placing a copper disc on an axle with wires touching the edge of the disc and the axle, and connected to a galvanometer. The disc was situated between two poles of a powerful horsehoe magnet. When the disc rotated, electric current was induced.

Faraday wrote down how he set up and performed his experiments. In November 1831, he reported his results to the Royal Society. In his paper, he developed two laws from his experiments:

1. When there is magnetic flux through a circuit, an electromotive force (the force that pushes electric current) is induced in the circuit.

*The title page of the first edition of Michael Faraday's* Experimental Researches in Electricity

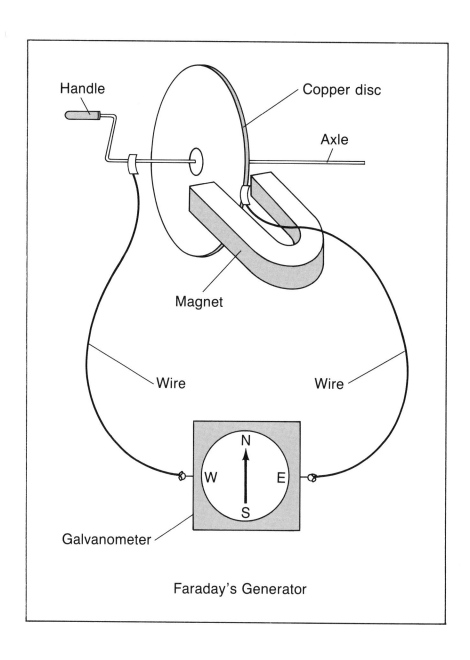

Handle

Copper disc

Axle

Magnet

Wire

Wire

N

W        E

S

Galvanometer

Faraday's Generator

2. The strength of this electromotive force is directly proportional to the rate of change in the magnetic flux.

A moving magnet may induce electric current, and how much current is determined by how fast or slowly the magnet changes the fields of force.

The scientists of the Royal Society accepted Faraday's work with enthusiasm. He had invented the electric generator, or *dynamo.* His discovery of electromagnetic induction paved the way for changing mechanical energy into electrical energy.

Faraday had come up with a new idea of energy. He discovered that the movement of a magnet may cause current in a wire. The movement is mechanical energy and, when this movement causes current, it is converted to electrical energy. Faraday's experiment proved that current is the result of the motion of a conductor interacting with a magnetic field.

Faraday's disc experiment turned out to be the first direct current dynamo. It was the first device to change mechanical energy into a steady electric current.

Electric generators today, based upon Faraday's experiment of some 150 years ago, power the world. Today, more electricity is produced by Faraday's methods than by any other means. There are other ways of producing electricity: batteries; thermocouples, by using heat; photoelectric cells, by using light. All of these methods are used today, but the electricity produced by all of them together does not equal the amount produced by Faraday's generator.

Generators run by water power (hydroelectric power), by coal, by oil, and by nuclear energy provide electric power. All of the generators work on the principle of converting mechanical energy into electrical energy. This electrical energy goes out from the power station and is again converted into other forms of energy when it reaches the homes, businesses, and industries it is destined for.

*An engraving of Michael Faraday lecturing
to children on the generation of electricity*

# JOSEPH HENRY

It seems that most great discoveries in science have been duplicated because more than one person was working on the same
idea independently of another. This is not so surprising if you
consider that research is based on what is known at a particular
time. In the 1800s, people were fascinated by electricity and magnetism.

Joseph Henry (1797–1878) was born in Albany, New York, to
parents of Scottish ancestry. As a child, he lived with his grand-
mother in the country, where he attended the local school. When
he was ten, he took a job at a village store and attended school
only half time, but he spent all his free time reading. He loved
books and could often be found reading at the library.

When Henry was fifteen, his father died, and the young man
moved back to Albany to live with his mother, who ran a boarding
house. Henry was quite interested in acting and thought that his
future lay in an acting career. He wrote plays and spent much
time backstage at the Albany Theater watching the actors from
New York who came to entertain in local productions.

At sixteen, Henry had an accident, and received an injury to
his face. This confined him to the house for some time. While
recovering, something happened that changed the direction of
his life.

Henry came upon a book one of his mother's boarders was
reading. The book was entitled *Lectures on Experimental Philosophy, Astronomy, and Chemistry,* by a Dr. Gregory.

Dr. Gregory's book opened an entire new world to Henry,
who had never been exposed to science before. He found the
subject fascinating and challenging. As a result, he left all ideas of
acting behind to become a student and, soon after, a teacher.

In 1824, Henry joined the Albany Institute. Like the Royal
Institution in London, England, the Albany Institute was com-
posed of men of science, and served as a forum for sharing
research through lectures and scientific papers. Henry gave his

first demonstration to the Institute in 1824, the year he joined. His experiment was on the elasticity of steam. Three years later, in 1827, Henry presented his first paper on electricity. The subject was electromagnetism, and the paper described the work of William Sturgeon, the London scientist who had made the first electromagnet.

Henry's research led him to experiment with magnets. He began to build electromagnets in which he wound coils of insulated wire around horseshoe-shaped iron cores. As the research continued, Henry, along with an assistant, Philip Ten Eyck, built a magnet capable of lifting a ton of iron. Henry called his magnets "intensity magnets," because they consisted of many coils of wire.

Henry's experimentation with magnets led him to electromagnetic induction and induction theory. If electricity produces magnetism, then magnetism should be able to produce electricity, he theorized.

Henry set up a coiled electromagnetic apparatus near a second coil, which he attached to a galvanometer. His results were the same as Faraday's. When the circuit was closed, there was a momentary deflection of the galvanometer needle. When the circuit was broken, the needle deflected in the other direction. Henry concluded that it was the changing magnetic field which caused the deflections to occur. The current occurs because of a change in the magnetic intensity.

*Joseph Henry in the United States discovered induction at about the same time as Faraday discovered it. In later years, Joseph Henry became the first director of the Smithsonian Institution in Washington, D.C.*

Joseph Henry, working on induction on his own in America, did not know of Michael Faraday's work. He was shocked when he read of Faraday's researches in a scientific journal. Henry gave credit to Faraday for the discovery of induction. However, after 1832, each man's research took a different direction. Faraday served as a consultant to private companies and as a public lecturer. He was a very popular lecturer. One of his most famous lectures, "The Chemical History of a Candle," was for children and was given every Christmas.

Henry continued to research heavily into induction. In his experimentation, he found that a changing magnetic field around a conductor induced an opposing current to the original current in the same conductor. This is called self-induction.

Self-induction was a landmark discovery, for it set the stage for the development of the modern electric motor and generator. Without an understanding of self-induction, efficient motors and generators could not have been constructed.

Faraday also observed self-induction, but the discovery of this principle is credited to Henry. Today, the unit of self-induction is called a henry.

Henry also discovered the principle of the transformer. A transformer can increase or reduce varying electric voltages. Henry discovered this principle while experimenting with coils of wire placed at varying distances from one another. One of the modern applications of Henry's discovery is the induction coil used in today's automobiles. The induction coil increases low voltage.

In 1847, Henry was asked to become the first director of the Smithsonian Institution in Washington, D.C. Henry agreed, and spent the final years of his life shaping the Smithsonian's scope and direction.

# CHAPTER

# ELECTROMAGNETIC COMMUNICATION

The nineteenth century was a time of extensive research and important discoveries in the science of electricity. In laboratories throughout Europe and the United States, work went forward in induction, self-induction, electromagnetism, and other phenomena. One great mind would further the discoveries made by another great mind, only to have this work improved upon by yet another.

So it was that James Clerk Maxwell (1831-1879), a Scottish mathematician, worked on Faraday's theories. Maxwell, at the age of twelve, demonstrated a fantastic ability in mathematics and science. He was educated at Edinburgh Academy and at the University of Edinburgh. He then moved on to Cambridge, where he studied mathematics. During this time, Maxwell began to acquire knowledge of Faraday's work.

After reading Faraday's *Experimental Researches,* he translated Faraday's ideas into mathematical expression. Maxwell, who has been called the greatest theoretical physicist of the nineteenth century, made an important contribution to the field of electrical theory. Many of the electrical advances of today were made possible by Maxwell's computations in the 1800s.

# THE DEVELOPMENT
# OF THE TELEGRAPH

Stephen Gray's discovery of the transmission of electricity over conducting threads probably stimulated the idea of electronic communication. Oersted's discovery of electromagnetism also stimulated research into communication. Ampère proposed an electromagnetic telegraph that would use coils and magnetic needles, and Joseph Henry, in 1831, designed the first electromagnetic telegraph.

All of these ideas and inventions led to the modern telegraph, brought to public light in 1839 by Samuel F. B. Morse.

Samuel Finlay Breese Morse (1791-1872) was a landscape and portrait painter and one of the founders of the National Academy of Design. He became interested in electricity in 1827, while taking some courses at Columbia College in New York City. During this time, he studied electromagnetism under the supervision of James F. Dana, a professor at the college. But Morse's great love was his art, and the study of electromagnetism only an interesting pastime.

In 1829, Morse left the United States for a five-year tour of Europe to study the great works of European artists. He studied in France, England, and Italy.

It was on his return voyage home that Morse met Charles S. Jackson. Jackson described some of the electrical experiments he had seen in Paris. This conversation renewed Morse's interest in electromagnetism, and he began to think about ideas for an electric telegraph. While still on the voyage, he worked out a design on paper for an electromagnetic telegraph apparatus and a code for sending messages.

*Samuel F. B. Morse is shown
in this painting with his
invention, the telegraph.*

Upon his return to the United States, Morse went to live with his brother, Richard. Richard provided Morse with the space and the funds to complete his work on the telegraph. Morse designed a telegraph that would send and receive messages mechanically. The work went very slowly, and Morse eked out a living by painting portraits.

In 1835, Morse was given a professorship at New York City University. It was on this campus that he enlisted the help of a physician/physicist and inventor named Page. Page helped Morse work out the last problems with his system and also helped him to design an electrical relay device. The relay was suggested by Joseph Henry.

In September of 1834, Morse demonstrated his telegraph operating through 1700 feet (518 m) of wire. As a result he received some financial backing from the United States Government, but not enough to establish any lines for operation. It took many more years of demonstrations until, on December 30, 1842, the Congress of the United States appropriated $30,000 for an experimental line between Washington, D.C. and Baltimore, Maryland.

It was not until May 24, 1844, that the line was finally finished and ready to be tested. Morse sent the first message—"What hath God wrought"—from Washington to Baltimore, and the operator in Baltimore repeated the message back to Morse.

In June, 1846, a telegraph line was installed between New York City and Washington, D.C. By 1848, independently-owned telegraph lines were spreading all over the United States. In 1851, there were over fifty telegraph companies. By 1856, Morse organized his own Magnetic Telegraph Company and, under the Western Union System, combined many of the smaller companies into one.

THE TELEPHONE

The development of the telegraph paved the way for an even more significant invention. If coded messages could be sent over wire via electromagnetism, why couldn't actual speech be transmitted? It was only a matter of time before the idea was perfected.

Many scientists were stimulated by the idea of being able to talk over long distances. As with electromagnetic induction and the telegraph, several people worked independently on the idea of a telephone at the same time, each working without knowledge of what the others were doing.

In 1854 a Frenchman named Charles Bourseul published an article on the electrical transmission of speech. In this article, Bourseul described a device he had designed that was capable of transmitting the human voice. Although Bourseul did not actually build this device, his theories excited the scientific community.

Seven years later, a German, Johann Philipp Reis (1834-1874), published an article describing a device which he had built. He called the contraption a telephone and, in his article, described its operating procedures. Reis's telephone was modeled after Bourseul's idea. The telephone was made up of a *transmitter*, which was a stretched membrane to which a metallic device was attached at its center. As someone would speak into the transmitter, the voice would trigger the opening and closing of an electrical circuit leading to the *receiver*. This receiver was an electromagnetic device attached to a metal diaphragm (thin disc).

There is no doubt that both Bourseul and Reis had the right idea, but the telephones they designed did not have the ability to reproduce speech accurately. The opening and closing of the circuit produced only a buzz at the receiver. Neither of these men knew that in order to produce sound, the electric signals had to be modulated to imitate the human voice.

Work progressed on the idea of transmitting speech. A man named Elisha Gray filed a patent for a telephone on February 14, 1876. Gray's telephone went further than the Reis device in that it varied the resistance in the telephone circuit, thus modulating the voice patterns.

On the same day that Gray submitted his application for a patent, Alexander Graham Bell also submitted a patent for a telephone. Each man had worked independently of the other, and each had filed for a patent without knowledge that the other had done the same.

## ALEXANDER GRAHAM BELL

Alexander Graham Bell (1847-1922) was born in Scotland, and grew up in a family that was interested and involved in the science of sound. Both Bell's grandfather and father taught speech to the deaf and to people with speech impairments. As a boy, Bell made a talking doll that could say "mama."

Bell became a professor of vocal physiology, and founded the Volta Bureau, an organization devoted to increasing the understanding of deafness. He moved to Canada in 1870 and to the United States in 1872. Later, he became a United States citizen, and did most of his important work in this country.

In Boston, Massachusetts, Bell searched for a way of sending many messages at once over a telegraph. By accident, he discovered that sound could cause an electromagnet to move thin strips of steel. Bell worked on his discovery for a year. In 1876, a human voice was transmitted over a wire for the first time. Bell had invented the first practical telephone.

Here is how the device was designed to work. When a person speaks into a telephone, an electric current is generated by the vibrations. These electronic vibrations are then carried over a wire to a receiver. The transmitter contains a metal diaphragm

*Alexander Graham Bell in 1892 at the New York end of the first long-distance telephone call to Chicago*

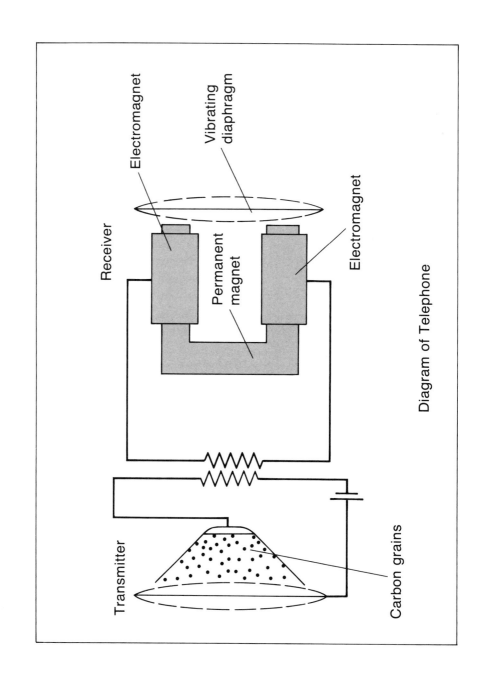

Receiver

Electromagnet

Vibrating diaphragm

Permanent magnet

Electromagnet

Transmitter

Carbon grains

Diagram of Telephone

sensitive to these vibrations. This metal disc, called a diaphragm, vibrates at different speeds in response to different sounds.

The diaphragm is connected to a cup filled with tiny grains of carbon. These carbon grains make it possible to mimic the exact sound of the voice. A loud sound pushes the grains tightly together, and makes it easier for an electric current to travel over the wire. The grains remain less compact with softer sounds, and make it more difficult for the current to travel over the wire.

The sound waves themselves do not travel through the wire. The sound waves disturb the steady flow of the regular electrical current. It is this disturbance that duplicates the waves from a speaker's voice. The disturbed current travels through the wire, and is again transformed into sound waves at the receiver.

The receiver is made of a diaphragm that vibrates on electrical impulse. Two magnets on the side of the diaphragm cause it to vibrate. One of the magnets is a permanent magnet (a magnet that is always magnetized); the other is an electromagnet (a magnet that is magnetized by an electric current). The permanent magnet keeps the diaphragm in place and close to the permanent magnet. The electromagnet controls the vibrations of the diaphragm by pulling it away from or pushing it toward the permanent magnet.

As one speaks into the transmitter of a telephone, the voice patterns cause the carbon particles to change the resistance in the circuits. This resistance controls the amount of current passing through the wires. According to the amount of current, the electromagnet in the receiver becomes weaker or stronger, and either pushes or pulls on the diaphragm. This vibration occurs at the same frequency as the sound waves that enter the transmitter. Therefore, the human voice is almost exactly duplicated.

Your telephone is part of a worldwide communications system. When you make a call, the signal travels to a switching station. Here, the switching apparatus connects your telephone to the telephone at the number you are calling. All this happens with amazingly rapid speed.

As you pick up your telephone, a dial tone signals that the circuits are clear to handle your call. Dialing your number breaks the current, and an electric signal goes to electromagnets that connect you to the number you have dialed.

Over 100 million telephones are in use today all over the world, over half of them in the United States. Who would have thought that in just over one hundred years the art of communication would have come this far?

CHAPTER

# THE DEVELOPMENT OF THE ELECTRIC LIGHT

The first idea for an electric light probably started with Sir Humphry Davy's electric arc in 1809. Many carbon arc lights were designed to light up the darkened streets of cities.

The arc light worked by an arc of electricity jumping between two carbon rods. But there were problems. The arc light required a great deal of power and, until the mid-1800s, there was no battery powerful enough to sustain the light's glow. The other problem was that the carbon rods rapidly burned away and, as they burned, they had to be readjusted.

## PRACTICAL USES OF ARC LIGHTING

After Faraday's discovery of electromagnetic induction and the later development of the dynamo, electric lighting became more practical. The first dynamo used for electric lighting was at South Foreland Lighthouse in England. It was an arc light powered by a Nollet magnetogenerator. The arc lamp worked by an electric current flowing between the two conductors, or electrodes. The arc occurs because the air between the two electrodes is ionized (broken down), and this ionized air acts as a conductor for the current.

In 1876, a Russian named Paul Jablochkov invented a practical arc lamp he called the Jablochkov candle. This light was the first to operate on an alternating current generator. By using alternating current (AC), both carbon rods burned evenly at the same speed. The Jablochkov candle gave off a soft, steady light.

In 1878, Charles Francis Brush (1849–1929) installed twenty arc lamps in Wanamaker's department store in Philadelphia. These lights were powered by the Brush dynamo. In 1879, arc lights powered by Brush dynamos lit up Cleveland's public square.

By 1885, arc lighting for the streets of America and Europe was common. However, although arc lighting served well for outdoor use, it was not well suited for indoor illumination. People preferred the soft light of the gas lamp indoors to the constantly flickering arc lamp.

## THE INCANDESCENT LAMP

The *incandescent lamp* was attempted by Sir Humphry Davy as early as 1809. An incandescent lamp is one in which a wire is heated until it glows. The major drawback in developing this type of lamp was that the wires burned out very rapidly. It was theorized that if the wires were heated in an airless state (vacuum), they would last longer.

In 1841, an Englishman named Frederick de Moleyns applied for a patent for an incandescent lamp. In developing the lamp he attempted to remove the air from an enclosed globe so the wire could burn longer at a higher temperature.

An American named Starr, in 1845, along with an Englishman named Kiry, applied for a patent for two incandescent lamps. Both of these lamps worked in a vacuum globe but, again, their life span was too short for the lamps to be of practical use.

It was in 1860 that Joseph Wilson Swan (1828-1914), an

Englishman, developed an incandescent lamp using a horse-shoe-shaped filament. (A filament is the wire that glows in an incandescent lamp.) The main problem with his lamp was having enough of a vacuum so that the lamp would not burn out.

The breakthrough occurred in 1865, when Hermann Johann Philipp Sprengel (1834–1906) invented a vacuum pump that was able to remove almost all of the air from the globes of these incandescent lamps. After Sprengel's pump was put into use, Swan worked on making more efficient incandescent lamps. He finally succeeded in 1878.

Many people argue that it is Swan, not Thomas Edison, who deserves credit for the invention of the incandescent light. But Edison was well on his way when Swan finally perfected his lamp. Edison's goal was a complete system for lighting an entire city, including a power plant.

## THOMAS EDISON

Thomas Alva Edison (1847-1931) was one of the most well-known inventors of all time. Self-educated, Edison became interested in chemistry and electronics. His inquisitiveness caused him to experiment in both of these fields, and some of his experiments got him into trouble. One time he set a baggage car on fire while experimenting with the chemical phosphorus.

Eventually Edison found a job as a telegraph operator in Mt. Clemens, Michigan. Among his duties was the task of reporting, by telegraph, to the city of Toronto. He had to do this hourly. Edison viewed this reporting as a waste of valuable time, so he rigged up a time clock and attached a telegraph set to it. The time clock triggered the telegraph, and a signal was sent to Toronto hourly. This was Edison's first invention, and led to him spending almost all of his time working on other innovations.

Edison opened his first workshop in Menlo Park, New Jersey, where he developed many devices to help business and industry.

Among these were improvement of the stock ticker; the carbon telephone transmitter; and the electric pen, which was used on the first mimeograph machine. Edison also contributed to film making, and was instrumental in the development of sound movies.

One of Edison's most original inventions was the phonograph. He developed this idea while attempting to find a way to record telegraph messages.

It is apparent that the incandescent light was not Edison's exclusive idea but, as he did with the telephone and the stock ticker, Edison found a way of making this device more practical. What Edison was looking for was a safer and more efficient light that could be used in homes and industries. In order to accomplish this, he needed to move away from gas as the source of energy.

Edison's efforts finally paid off in 1879. After many unsuccessful attempts, he discovered a way to keep a filament glowing. He had tried almost every kind of material in his electric light, but nothing had worked. Finally, he tried carbonized thread, a thread coated with a carbon material. This, he thought, might work because it contained no oxygen. After many tries, he succeeded in placing the thread in a bulb. The bulb burned for approximately twenty-four hours.

Today, the incandescent light bulb produces a bright and steady light for many hours by means of electricity. The bulb itself has a positive and negative contact on its base. Wires run through the base and into the bulb. These wires, called lead-in wires, are attached to a filament generally made of tungsten. The bulb itself is usually filled with an inert gas (a gas that is chemically inactive) in order to keep oxygen out. Oxygen would make the filament burn out.

The filament in the electric light is usually a long, coiled, thin wire. (The longer the wire, the greater the electrical resistance. Also, the thinner the wire, the greater the resistance.) Electrical

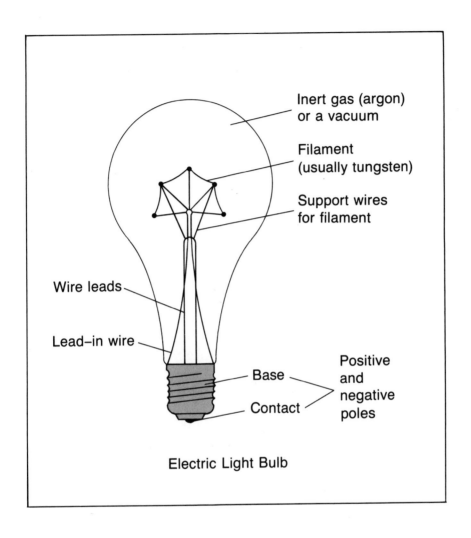

Inert gas (argon)
or a vacuum

Filament
(usually tungsten)

Support wires
for filament

Wire leads

Lead–in wire

Base

Contact

Positive
and
negative
poles

Electric Light Bulb

resistance produces heat. As the electric current moves through the filament, free electrons bounce off the atoms. This creates friction and heat. The filament glows.

# CHAPTER

# THE DEVELOPMENT
# OF FARADAY'S
# DYNAMO

After Faraday's discovery of the electric motor and generator, the development of other electric motors and generators proceeded in a burst of scientific activity. Electric motors came first. This was because there was a power source, the voltaic cell. It was actually a twofold process: the development of power sources and the development of electric motors. The ratio was: the greater the source of power, the more efficient and powerful the electric motor.

It was two years after Faraday's discovery of induction that a Russian, Hermann Jacobi, built an electric motor that was powerful enough to move a paddle-wheel boat carrying fourteen passengers.

Even before Jacobi, William Sturgeon built a small electric motor that served as the original model for many of the electrical motors built later. Joseph Henry also built an electric motor. In 1839, a Scottsman, Robert Davidson, built a motor that operated a lathe and a small electric cart.

By the 1880s, electric motors were in common use in Europe and the United States. There were motors for all sorts of functions. The mechanical revolution had begun.

The electric generator, or dynamo, took longer to perfect. There were many mechanical problems that had to be solved before the generation of electricity would be practical. As usual, several people worked independently to solve these problems of electromagnetic induction for power.

Electromagnetism is magnetism produced by an electric current. Electromagnetic induction is the production of an electric current by magnetism. Both the electric motor and generator operate on the principle that like poles repel each other and unlike poles attract one another. The magnetic force in a dynamo is exerted by electromagnets changing electrical energy into motion.

## CHANGING MECHANICAL ENERGY
## INTO ELECTRICAL ENERGY

All generators (dynamos) change mechanical energy into electrical energy. Unlike the electric motor, which can use a battery as the source of power, a generator must be driven by some type of machine that produces mechanical energy. This device is called a prime mover. For example, steam is the prime mover for many of today's power plants. The steam turns turbines, which produce the mechanical energy needed to produce electricity.

Simply, a generator consists of powerful magnets called a field structure, and a wire loop called an armature. The armature turns inside the field structure. The connecting link to an outside circuit is made of slip rings and brushes.

As the armature turns, it cuts the lines of force in the field structure, creating an electric current. The electric current flows through the wire to the slip rings, which are attached to the shaft of the armature. Brushes, usually made of carbon, are attached to the slip rings and to an outside circuit. The electricity reaches its outside goal through the brushes.

## ALTERNATING CURRENT

The armature is always turning and, thus, cuts the lines of force downward and then upward or right and then left. Because of this, the current changes direction with each turn of the armature. The change in direction against the lines of force reverses the current. This is called *alternating current*, or AC. Many generators, including the ones that provide our homes with electricity, produce alternating current.

As the armature turns, it changes direction against the lines of force, reversing the current.

As the armature moves and changes direction, so does the current. When the armature moves downward, it cuts the lines of force in one direction, and the current moves out. Then the armature moves up and cuts the lines of force in an opposite direction, and the current moves in. As the armature turns between the two magnets, current is produced. As the armature moves in its circle, current flows one way and then the other with each half-circle turn.

As the armature spins, the current flow changes direction. When the armature is straight up and down, no current is produced. The most current is produced when the armature is parallel between each magnet.

## DIRECT CURRENT

There are also *direct current* (DC) generators. Direct current generators cause the current to move in only one direction. This is done through a device called a commutator. The commutator changes the AC current inside the generator to DC current as it travels out of the generator. This type of current, because it is steady, is best for automobiles, ships, and locomotives.

Along with the development of the battery, the generator was the answer for supplying power to the entire world but, in the beginning, there were problems. How could the efficiency be increased? The answer: develop a stronger magnet.

In 1860, in Florence, Italy, Antonio Pacinotti developed a slotted ring armature. This armature was a winged iron ring wrapped with many coils of wires. Each coil went to its own separate con-

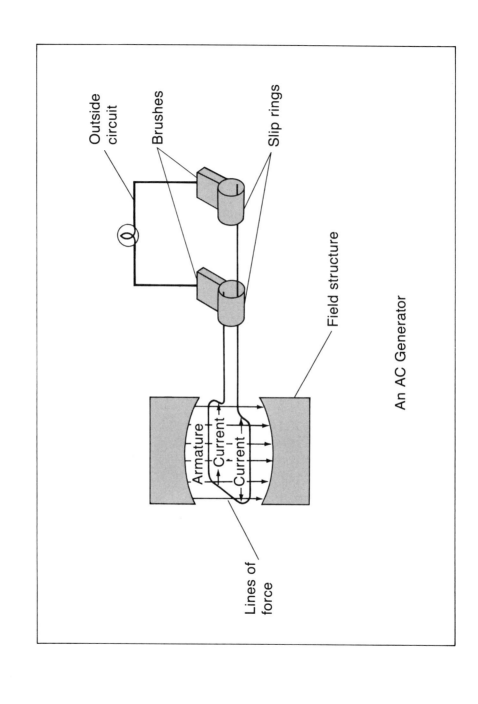

Outside circuit

Brushes

Slip rings

Field structure

Armature

Current

Current

Lines of force

An AC Generator

nection on the commutator. Pacinotti's device served as the model for almost all the generators to come.

Pacinotti's invention was improved upon by Zénobe Théophile Gramme (1826–1901), a Belgian. His invention was called the "Gramme Ring" armature. In 1873, one of Gramme's dynamoelectric machines accidentally caused a second machine, standing next to it, to speed up considerably. Gramme immediately knew the importance of this happening. He postulated that electricity could do much more work, that its power could be transported, by wire, all over the world.

## THE MODERN DYNAMO

Today, giant generators power our cities and industries, working on the same principles as those developed by Oersted, Faraday, Pacinotti, and Gramme. The field structure is an electromagnet that turns inside the armature. The armature is stationary, and the field structure turns.

Electric power plants use coal, oil, or water for many of their large generators. Coal is burned in a furnace and used to heat water into steam. The steam turns large blades of a turbine (prime mover). The turbine is connected to the shaft of an electromagnet (field structure), and causes it to turn inside the stationary armature. The spinning of the field structure produces electrical energy, alternating current (AC). Electric power lines that run to industries and homes are connected to the generator; the power that runs into homes lights rooms, runs appliances and sometimes heats the house.

# CHAPTER

# 7

## ELECTRONICS

In the twentieth century, developments in the science of electricity led investigators into the field of electronics. This is not to say that electronics supplanted electricity. In our modern world, there will always be uses for electricity, but the field of electronics has now become the emphasis for discovery. As with other major discoveries we have discussed, the key advances in electronics have been based on the independent researches of many people over a period of many years.

## THE SUBATOMIC WORLD

The term *electronics* takes its name from the electron, the negatively charged particle that orbits the nucleus of an atom. Perhaps the birth of electronics started with the realization, at the start of the nineteenth century, that the atom was not the smallest particle in nature. Scientists experimenting with electricity atoms in solutions observed how the atoms were altered. They were changed into electrically charged particles called *ions*. Humphry Davy and others theorized that because these atoms in solution changed into other charged particles, the atom itself must be made up of smaller particles that it either loses or gains. It was Faraday who named these charged particles ions (see next page).

Many atoms lose or gain electrons. An atom that loses electrons is a positive ion because it has more protons than electrons. If an atom gains an electron, it is a negative ion because it has more electrons than protons.

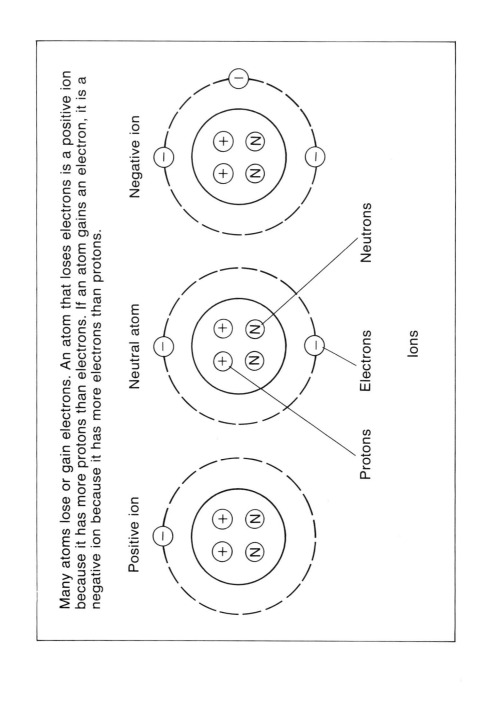

Positive ion

Neutral atom

Negative ion

Protons

Electrons

Neutrons

Ions

# THE EDISON EFFECT

A discovery very important to the development of electronics was made by Edison. It is referred to as the Edison effect. One problem Edison had with his light bulbs was that they blackened around the filament and near the positive terminal. In attempting to solve this problem, he placed a metal plate in one of his bulbs near the filament that was connected to the input wire. He discovered that when a battery was connected to both the filament and the plate, the current would only flow in one direction. He also noted that the filament gave off a blue glow. This "one way valve" that Edison discovered and patented became known as the Edison effect. Although Edison himself found no practical use for his Edison effect, it was a major discovery. Today, it is called the thermionic diode, and is the basis for the operation of all electron tubes.

# X-RAYS

It was in the 1890s that the field of electronics began to gain headway. In Germany, Wilhelm Konrad Roentgen (1845-1923), a professor of physics at Wurzburg University, discovered X-rays. He was in his laboratory performing some experiments with a vacuum tube when he noticed that a nearby screen, coated with barium platinocyanide, glowed as the tube was operating. A *vacuum tube* is a sealed glass tube or bulb from which almost all the air has been removed and into which electrodes from the outside project.

Roentgen experimented further, and discovered that objects placed between the tube and the screen formed an image on the screen, with the more dense objects casting darker shadows. It was not until several years later that scientists decided that Roentgen's X-rays were really electromagnetic waves.

A Frenchman, Jean Baptiste Perrin (1870–1942), about the time of Roentgen's discovery, found that the rays in a vacuum

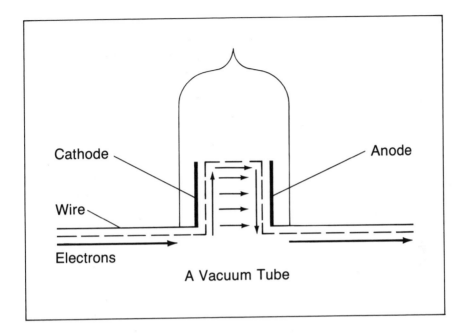

Cathode

Anode

Wire

Electrons

A Vacuum Tube

tube consisted of negatively charged particles. In 1898, in England, Joseph John Thomson (1856–1940) confirmed Perrin's discovery, and added that these rays were actually a stream of negatively charged particles. All of this came from a vacuum tube.

## ELECTRON TUBES

In vacuum tubes, electrons escape from their atoms, and a device called an *anode* attracts them, and a device called a *cathode* repels them. Magnetic fields are used to deflect the electrons as they travel through the vacuum. Once an electric field has

*Thomas Edison, photographed in 1915 with his "Edison effect" lamps*

been produced, it not only deflects electrons, but it also accelerates their movement. As electrons pass through an electric field, their speed is increased to near that of the speed of light. Tubes, transistors, and microchips control electrons in the above manner, and direct them to operate a specific electrical device.

Magnets, or magnetic fields, are used in electron tubes to direct the flow of electrons. Electrons are negatively charged. When electrons escape from the metal atoms, they are attracted by the anode, an electrode made positive, and pushed away from the cathode; the negative electrode. The electric current (flux) produces a magnetic field. The electric charges produce an applied field. This applied field is what causes the electrons to move almost as fast as the speed of light, while the magnetic field deflects electrons and controls their flow.

In certain types of devices, it is very important for the electrons to flow in a certain direction. Electron tubes, through the above-described process, control the stream of electrons.

As you have learned previously, electrons that travel through a wire create an electric current. When the current flows from start to finish, it is called a complete circuit. An electron tube is a break in the circuit. This tube, or transistor, interrupts the regular flow of electrons through the circuit. It becomes part of the circuit and controls the flow of electrons.

The electrons flow through the wire to the cathode across the tube from the anode. The tube has altered the current in some way to do a specific job. Perhaps it has speeded up the electron flow, or perhaps it has changed the direction of the flow. Whatever the tube did, the electrons, when they exit through the anode, are altered or have been altered in the tube.

Electron tubes and transistors can do many jobs: They rectify the current, changing alternating current to direct current. They amplify the current, increasing a small amount of current to a large amount. They convert electrical energy, changing current into X-rays or radio waves, for example.

# USING ELECTRICITY
# FOR COMMUNICATION

The early 1900s saw the development and increased efficiency of the vacuum tube. People such as Hertz, Marconi, De Forest, and Fleming worked on theories to make the output of electrons stronger and more efficient.

Heinrich Rudolf Hertz (1857-1894) laid the groundwork for the vacuum tube. He was one of the first people to demonstrate the existence of electric waves. Hertz actually produced these waves, and showed that they could be focused, reflected, and refracted.

In the early years of his career, Hertz was an assistant to Hermann Ludwig von Helmholtz (1821–1894) in Berlin, Germany. He was greatly influenced by both Helmholtz and James Clerk Maxwell (1831–1879). Their researches convinced Hertz that there were electromagnetic waves in space. In 1887, Hertz proved the existence of these waves.

Hertz set up a small experiment to prove his theories. At one end of a long table he set up an apparatus which consisted of an induction coil, a wire loop, and a spark gap. At the other end of the table he set up a lone spark gap attached to a circuit. An electrical discharge from the induction coil went across the gap at one end of the table and almost simultaneously sent a spark across the gap at the other end of the table.

After Hertz's discovery of electromagnetic waves, an Italian named Guglielmo Marconi (1874-1937) became interested in utilizing these waves for communication. After several years of experimentation, Marconi was finally able to send messages without wires over a distance of approximately one mile. By 1901, wireless signals could be sent over great distances. Marconi had invented the first radio.

In the United States, Lee De Forest (1873-1961) discovered that by placing a grid in a vacuum tube, he could control the Edi-

35

son effect. His discovery enhanced the development of radio and long distance telephone communication. De Forest's grid was placed in a three-element tube he called an *audion*. This *triode* tube was the first electronic amplifier.

Sir John Ambrose Fleming, an Englishman, was the first person to utilize the Edison effect in a *rectifier*. A rectifier is a device that allows current to flow in only one direction. Fleming adapted an Edison bulb by surrounding part of the filament with a metal cylinder which was connected to a separate terminal. He called his device the Fleming valve.

These discoveries of the early 1900s reached fruition with the development of radio broadcasting. After World War I, the advances in electronics were mainly geared to the entertainment and communication fields. It was not until after World War II that new developments began to take place.

## TELEVISION

The development of television had its beginnings in the mid-1800s, when some scientists attempted to send light images over a wire. Some researchers also experimented with discs that would spin over pictures to give the idea of moving images.

In 1908, an Englishman named Campbell-Swinton actually described the workings for a television. He theorized that the cathode ray from a vacuum tube could put an image on a fluorescent screen. In the 1920s, Vladimir Zworykin, a Russian who lived in the United States, and John Baird worked with the concept of television, utilizing a combination of electricity and electronics. But it was not until the late 1940s and early 1950s that television came into its own.

*Marconi sends the first wireless
marine message in America in 1899.*

Today's television sets use electronics to convert electrical energy into an electron beam. This conversion is performed by a cathode ray tube, which is located at the rear of a television picture tube.

The cathode rays beam electrons, which flow across the television screen. Whenever the electrons make contact with the fluorescent material on the screen, the screen lights up.

Electron beams light up dots on the television screen. These dots are made of phosphorus. As an electron beam touches a dot, it lights up. Only one dot at a time is lit by the electron beam, but the beam moves so rapidly that to the human eye the illuminated dots create a picture on the screen.

## THE TRANSISTOR

In the late 1940s, scientists working with the *semiconductor* silicon discovered that there were two types of this material, a positive (P) and a negative (N). They further discovered that when these two types of *silicon* met, they would transform (change) light energy into electricity. They could also act as a rectifier by changing AC current to DC current.

The discoveries of these properties of silicon were the first steps in the development of the transistor. On December 23, 1947, three scientists—William O. Shockley, Walter H. Brattain, and John Bardeen—were working with a *germanium* crystal (a semiconductor). When they placed two very tiny wires 2/1000 of an inch apart in order to make contact with the crystal, they discovered a telephone voice in the laboratory was amplified forty times.

What Shockley, Bardeen, and Brattain had discovered with crystals became known as the *transistor effect.* In 1956, these three men received the Nobel Prize in physics for their invention of the transistor.

The first transistors did not work very well. It was difficult to insert wires in the crystals and they were very noisy. This was because the silicon and germanium crystals used were filled with microscopic impurities.

A better method for refining silicon and germanium was discovered by William G. Pfann, a scientist working for Bell Laboratories. His method seemed to remove almost all of the impurities. Using Pfann's method, transistors of high quality were produced in 1955. The transistor industry boomed, as transistors replaced the vacuum tube in almost all electronic devices.

Transistors have many advantages over vacuum tubes. A vacuum tube is large and bulky, breaks easily, and is very slow. Transistors are small (today's transistors are microscopic), almost unbreakable, extremely fast, and consume little power.

Transistors also work in solid materials, while tubes must work in a vacuum. Any transistorized device is referred to as *solid state*, which indicates that it has no tubes.

Because transistors do not need a vacuum and because they run cool (do not heat up), they can be enclosed in a very small space. The use of transistors has led to the reduction in size of many devices. For example, a portable radio that used to weigh twenty-five pounds (11 kg) is now less than a pound.

Today, transistors are so small that a microscope is necessary to see them. Tens of thousands of transistors can fit into one microchip that may be no bigger than the eraser on a number two pencil. When transistors are packed together in a tiny chip, it is called an *integrated circuit*. An electronic device may have many integrated circuits connected by etching, not wires. Etching is like scratching on the surface, or a groove.

Integrated circuits are found in television sets, radios, tape recorders, cameras, automobiles, aircraft, computers, satellites, and space shuttles.


MICROELECTRONICS

By the late 1950s, the need for very lightweight electrical circuits became apparent as the world began to move into the space age.

Scientists began to work on such devices. The field of *microelectronics* was born.

Microelectronics utilizes very tiny electron devices called integrated circuits to run very lightweight, sophisticated, and compact equipment. Today, a computer the size of a typewriter, containing microprocessors made up of thousands of transistors and other devices, performs operations that once would have needed a very large room full of equipment.

Some computers run by microprocessers are even smaller than a typewriter. There are computers so small that they can fit into your pocket. There are computers the size of a pencil head that run wristwatches. Not only have these computers decreased in size, but they have also, because they are very accurate, decreased the margin of error.

# CHAPTER

## TO SOLAR GENERATORS

Most of the energy on Earth comes from the sun. It is this solar energy, produced by atomic reactions inside the sun, that creates the energy stored beneath the surface of our planet. The type of atomic reaction that occurs inside the sun is called nuclear *fusion*. In fusion, the atom implodes (crushes). This crushing of the atom creates a chain reaction in which millions of other atoms are crushed. The major result of this type of massive fusion reaction is the release of tremendous amounts of heat and light energy.

Another type of atomic energy is *fission*, the splitting of the atom. When an atom is split, it splits other atoms, causing a chain reaction that releases heat and light.

Some of our electric power plants now are run by nuclear fission. They are called atomic power plants. In atomic power plants, *uranium* atoms are used as fuel. Through a special process, the uranium atom is split, setting off a chain reaction in which millions of atoms split. This is fission. The heat energy from fission is used to make steam, and the steam turns the turbines of the electrical generators.

Scientists today are working on the development of a fusion generator. Fusion is a much safer type of nuclear reaction because it does not give off any deadly radiation. Also, the fuel for a fusion reaction is *deuterium*. The supply of deuterium is virtually inexhaustible.

The goal of much energy research today is to capture solar energy directly from the sun to create steam to turn the turbines of power plants. But the sun's energy is elusive. Energy that reaches our Earth is spread out over a vast area. In order for us to use the energy of the sun, it must be concentrated. Solar collectors have been developed to store the energy of the sun. These collectors are flat plates that absorb the sun's energy and store it in heated water. These solar collectors may eventually be refined to produce enough energy to run an electric power plant.

The most practical use today for solar energy is in our space program. It is solar energy that provides most of the power for all of the satellites that have been sent up to orbit Earth. This is accomplished through *solar cells*, or solar batteries.

Solar cells, or batteries, convert light energy into electricity. These cells consist of layers of silicon or germanium that capture the energy of the sun and turn it into a constant and reliable electric source. On Earth, panels of solar cells facing the sun have been used to supply electric power to buildings and schools. This use, however, is still not common; most solar cells today are used to heat water.

As our scientists find more efficient ways to collect, concentrate, and store solar energy, it is possible that the sun may become the main source of energy on the planet Earth. This solar energy could be used for heating and cooling homes and schools and for efficiently running generators that would provide enough electricity to power an entire city.

Electricity was discovered thousands of year ago. Today, its use is still being refined and redesigned to make a better world for us. In our modern society, energy is the most valuable commodity. People need energy to run all of the complicated systems of today's world. As human beings advance into the future, electrical energy will play a major role in the development of technologies to come. It will take more people like Faraday, Galvani, and the others mentioned in this book, people who will dare to advance new theories. Only through new ideas, presented by courageous persons, can the destiny of the human race be fulfilled.

# GLOSSARY

ALTERNATING CURRENT (AC). An electrical current in which the electricity flows regularly in one direction and then the other, reversing many times per second. Most electrical generators produce alternating current.

ANODE. The positive (+) pole of an electron tube or battery. Negatively charged ions are attracted to the anode.

ATOM. A small particle that makes up matter. All atoms have a positively charged nucleus containing protons and neutrons, and negatively charged orbits.

AUDION. A triode device.

CATHODE. The negative (−) pole of an electron tube or battery. Positively charged ions are attracted to the cathode.

COMPASS. A device used to determine direction of a magnetic field, including Earth's. Consists of a magnetic needle which is free to turn under the influence of Earth's magnetic field.

CONDUCTOR. Any substance which has the ability to transmit an electrical charge. Copper and silver are good conductors of electricity.

CURRENT ELECTRICITY. Electrons moving through a conductor.

DEUTERIUM. The fuel used in a fusion reaction.

DIRECT CURRENT (DC). An electrical current whose electrons flow in one direction.

DYNAMO. An electric generator.

EDISON EFFECT. The flow of electrons from a heated wire to a nearby positively charged plate.

ELECTRIC ARC. An arc of light that occurs between two electrified carbon rods.

ELECTRICITY. A form of energy.

ELECTROLYSIS. The breaking down of a chemical compound in solution by passing an electric current through the solution.

ELECTROMAGNET. A device created by wrapping electrical wire around magnetic material and then passing a current through the wire.

ELECTROMAGNETIC INDUCTION. Producing an electric current by moving a conductor through a magnetic field or moving a magnetic field close to a conductor; main operating principle of electric generator and electric motors.

ELECTRON. The only moving part of an atom, possessing a negative (−) charge and moving in orbits around the nucleus.

ELECTRONICS. The study of electrons in motion.

FISSION (nuclear). The splitting of the atom to release heat and light energy.

FORCE. An influence that creates a push or pull on an object.

FUSION (nuclear). The imploding (crushing) of an atom to release heat and light energy.

GALVANOMETER. An instrument used for measuring an electric current.

GENERATOR. A device which converts mechanical energy into electrical energy.

GERMANIUM. A semiconductor material used in the production of transistors.

INCANDESCENT LAMP. A bulb which gives off light at a high temperature.

INTEGRATED CIRCUIT. Refers to circuits used in electronics on transistors and microchips.

ION. Any atom that possesses an electrical charge. An atom that has more protons than electrons is a positive ion; one with more electrons than protons is a negative ion.

MAGNETISM. A phenomenon involving attraction and repulsion. Also associated with electrical charges moving in a conductor or in electrical charges occurring in a field influenced by a magnet.

MICROELECTRONICS. The branch of electronics dealing with smaller than miniature.

NEGATIVE CHARGE. Any object with more electrons than protons has a negative charge.

POSITIVE CHARGE. Any object with more protons than electrons has a positive charge.

PROTON. The part of an atom, in the nucleus, that possesses a positive charge.

RECTIFIER. A device that allows an electric current to flow in only one direction. In electron tubes or solid state devices, rectifiers change alternating current to direct current.

SEMICONDUCTOR. A solid substance, such as silicon or germanium, whose electrical resistance decreases as its temperature increases.

SILICON. A nonmetallic element; in crystal form it is a semiconductor.

SOLAR CELL. A device that uses radiant energy from the sun to produce an electric current.

SOLAR COLLECTOR. A device that collects heat energy from the sun and stores it in attached water tanks or pipes.

SOLID STATE. Describing a device that has no moving parts, no tubes.

STATIC ELECTRICITY. Electricity at rest. Usually a large number of electrons in one place, not flowing as a current.

TELEPHONE RECEIVER. A device that contains an electromagnet that vibrates a metal disc to reproduce voice patterns.

TELEPHONE TRANSMITTER. A device that contains carbon particles that move and alter the flow of electrons in order to produce electrical impulses that relay sound.

TRANSISTOR. A small, solid-state device designed to replace the electron tube.

TRIODE. A vacuum tube incorporating three separate elements:

an anode, a cathode, and a grid that controls the flow of electrons from the anode to the cathode.

URANIUM. An element that is the main fuel for nuclear fission.

VACUUM TUBE. A device used to control the flow of electric currents.

VOLTAIC PILE. The first battery. It used chemical energy to create electricity.

# CHRONOLOGY

| DATE | PERSON | MAJOR DISCOVERY OR INVENTION |
|---|---|---|
| 600 BCE* | Thales of Miletus | Attempted to explain how amber, a resin, and its attractive powers worked. |
| 1600 CE** | William Gilbert | Worked with magnetism. He wrote *On the Loadstone and Magnetic Bodies and on the Great Magnet, the Earth.* He was the first European to use the term electricity. |
| 1600s | Robert Boyle | Experimented with static electricity. |
| 1660 | Otto von Guericke | Built a static electric machine and worked with the laws of attraction and repulsion. |

*BCE means before the Common Era
**CE means Common Era

| 1729 | Stephen Gray | Was the first to use wire to conduct an electrical charge. |
| 1733 | Charles Du Fay | Discovered the existence of two kinds of electricity, static and current. |
| 1746 | Benjamin Franklin | Was the first to use the terms positive and negative charge when referring to electricity. |
| 1785 | Charles Augustin de Coulomb | Worked out the laws of electrical attraction and repulsion. |
| 1791 | Luigi Galvani | Observed the effect of electricity in frogs' legs. Developed theory of animal electricity. |
| 1796 | Count Alessandro Volta | Invented the voltaic pile, the world's first battery. |
| 1801 | Sir Humphry Davy | Produced the electric arc. Isolated and named several previously unknown elements. |
| 1819 | Hans Christian Oersted | Discovered that current electricity creates a magnetic field. |
| 1820 | François Jean Arago | Discovered that an electric current can magnetize previously unmagnetized materials. |
| 1820 | André Marie Ampère | Paved the way for the development of the electric motor and generator by explaining how electric current is related to magnetism. |

| | | |
|---|---|---|
| 1820 | Jean Baptiste Biot | Worked out mathematical laws governing magnetism and electricity. |
| 1820 | Felix Savart | Worked out mathematical laws governing magnetism and electricity. |
| 1821 | Michael Faraday | Developed first electric motor while working on the principle of electromagnetic rotation. |
| 1825 | William Sturgeon | Produced first electromagnet. |
| 1827 | Georg Simon Ohm | Developed Ohm's law, a mathematical theory which deals with electrical resistance. |
| 1832 | Michael Faraday | Invented the first electric generator while working on the principle of electromagnetic induction. |
| 1832 | Joseph Henry | Worked on electromagnetism and induction. Discovered induction independently of Faraday. Discovered self-induction. |
| 1830s | James Clerk Maxwell | Translated Faraday's works into mathematical expression. |
| 1841 | Frederick de Moleyns | Applied for a patent for an incandescent lamp. |
| 1844 | Samuel F. B. Morse | Put first successful long distance telegraph into operation. |

| | | |
|---|---|---|
| 1845 | Starr and Kiry | Applied for patent for two incandescent globe-type lamps. |
| 1854 | Charles Bourseul | Described a device he designed that was capable of transmitting speech. |
| 1860 | Sir Joseph Wilson Swan | Developed an incandescent lamp using a horseshoe-shaped filament. |
| 1860 | Antonio Pacinotti | Developed slotted ring armature for generators. |
| 1861 | Johann Philipp Reis | Built a telephone using Bourseul's specifications. |
| 1865 | Hermann Johann Philipp Sprengel | Invented vacuum pump able to remove air from the globes of incandescent lamps. |
| 1873 | Zinoble Theophile Gramme | Invented an improved armature called the "Gramme ring." |
| 1876 | Elisha Gray | Filed a patent for a telephone. |
| 1876 | Alexander Graham Bell | Filed a patent for a telephone independently of Gray. |
| 1876 | Paul Jablochkov | Invented a practical arc lamp called the Jablochkov candle. |
| 1878 | Charles Francis Brush | Invented dynamo that powered twenty arc lights in a department store. |
| 1879 | Thomas Alva Edison | Applied for patent for incandescent lamp and opened first power station at Menlo Park, New Jersey. |

| 1887 | Heinrich Hertz | The first person to demonstrate the existence of electric waves. |
|------|----------------|------------------------------------------------------------------|
| 1895 | Wilhelm Konrad Roentgen | Discovered X-rays. |
| 1895 | Jean Perrin | Found the rays in a vacuum tube consisted of negatively charged particles. |
| 1895 | Joseph John Thomson | Confirmed Perrin's discovery and added that these were a stream of negatively charged particles. |
| 1901 | Guglielmo Marconi | Invented the first radio. |
| 1907 | Lee De Forest | Applied for a patent for his "audion," a triode tube. |
| 1908 | Sir John Ambrose Fleming | First to utilize the Edison effect in a rectifier. |
| 1908 | Campbell-Swinton | Described the workings for a television. |
| 1920 | Vladimir Zworykin | Worked with the concept of television. |
| 1920 | John Baird | Worked with the concept of television. |
| 1947 | William O. Shockley, John Bardeen, Walter H. Brattain | Invented the transistor. |
| 1955 | William C. Pfann | Found a way to remove impurities from semiconductors. |

# INDEX